Road Trip TRAVEL Journal

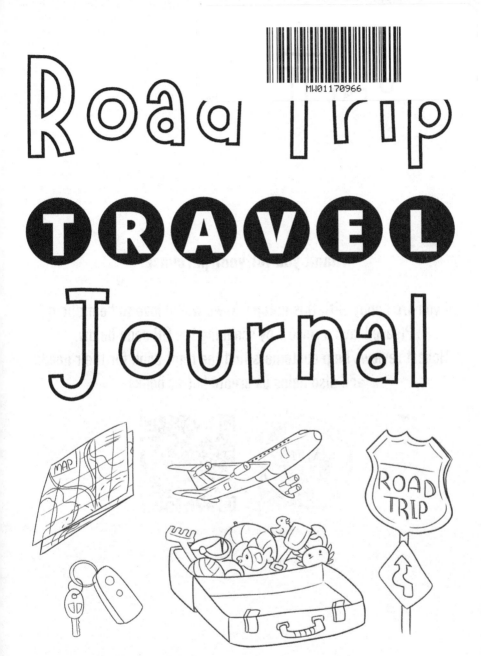

Thank you for your purchase!

If you are happy with this notebook, we would love to hear about it.
Please leave a review by scanning the QR code below.
Honest reviews help customers find the right book for their needs
and also helps us create better books.

let's go travel

THIS JOURNAL BELONGS TO:

_____

_____

_____

_____

_____

About Me

Today's date:_____

My name is:

_____

I am _____ years old.

My birthday is:

_____

My favorite:

Color: _____

Food: _____

Book: _____

Season: _____

Movie: _____

Trip # 1

Destination:

_____

_____

_____

_____

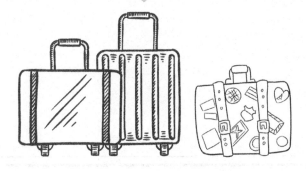

Before the trip...

Date:_____

What are you most excited about?

Make a list of the things you want to take on your trip:

- _____
- _____
- _____
- _____
- _____

Here are the people going with me!

Traveling...

Date:_____

Weather: ☀️ 🌈 ⛅ 🌧️ ⛈️ 🌨️

What I did today ...

_____
_____
_____
_____
_____
_____

What I loved about today...

_____
_____
_____
_____
_____
_____

Something new I tried or learned today...

_____
_____
_____
_____
_____

Mood:

Write, draw, and collect memories...

Date:_____

Draw, write or stick a ticket, a bill, a map, or anything else you collected from this trip...

After my trip...

Date:_____

How would you rate this trip?

Color the stars...

1 star - Didn't like the trip
2 stars - It was okay
3 stars - Had a fun trip
4 stars - Best trip ever!

Would you recommend this trip to a friend?

✓ Check one...

☐ Yes

☐ No

☐ Maybe

Trip # 2

Destination:

_____

_____

_____

_____

_____

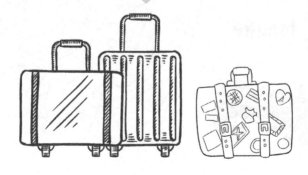

Before the trip...

Date:_____

What are you most excited about?

_____
_____
_____
_____

Make a list of the things you want to take on your trip:

- _____
- _____
- _____
- _____
- _____

Here are the people going with me!

Traveling...

Date:_____

Weather:

What I did today ...

What I loved about today...

Something new I tried or learned today...

Mood:

Write, draw, and collect memories...

Draw, write or stick a ticket, a bill, a map, or anything else you collected from this trip...

After my trip...

Date:_____

How would you rate this trip?

Color the stars...

1 star - Didn't like the trip
2 stars - It was okay
3 stars - Had a fun trip
4 stars - Best trip ever!

Would you recommend this trip to a friend?

✓ Check one...

☐ Yes
☐ No
☐ Maybe

Trip # 3

Destination:

_____

_____

_____

_____

_____

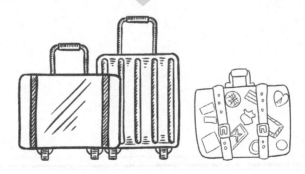

Before the trip...

Date:_____

What are you most excited about?

Make a list of the things you want to take on your trip:

- ----------------------------------
- ----------------------------------
- ----------------------------------
- ----------------------------------
- ----------------------------------

Here are the people going with me!

Traveling...

Weather:

What I did today ...

What I loved about today...

Something new I tried or learned today...

Mood:

Write, draw, and collect memories...

Date:_____

Draw, write or stick a ticket, a bill, a map, or anything else you collected from this trip...

After my trip...

Date:_____

How would you rate this trip?

Color the stars...

1 star - Didn't like the trip
2 stars - It was okay
3 stars - Had a fun trip
4 stars - Best trip ever!

Would you recommend this trip to a friend?

✓ Check one...

☐ Yes

☐ No

☐ Maybe

Trip # 4

Destination:

_____

_____

_____

_____

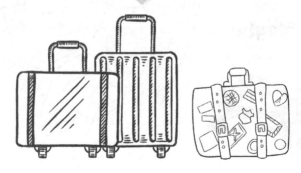

Before the trip...

Date:_____

What are you most excited about?

_____
_____
_____
_____

Make a list of the things you want to take on your trip:

- _____
- _____
- _____
- _____
- _____

Here are the people going with me!

Traveling...

Weather:

What I did today ...

What I loved about today...

Something new I tried or learned today...

Mood:

Date:_____

Draw, write or stick a ticket, a bill, a map, or anything else you collected from this trip...

After my trip...

Date:_____

How would you rate this trip?

Color the stars...

1 star - Didn't like the trip
2 stars - It was okay
3 stars - Had a fun trip
4 stars - Best trip ever!

Would you recommend this trip to a friend?

✓ Check one...

☐ **Yes**

☐ **No**

☐ **Maybe**

Trip # 5

Destination:

_____

_____

_____

_____

_____

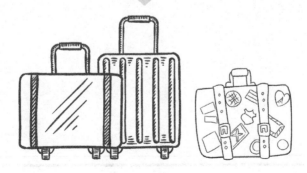

Before the trip...

Date:_____

What are you most excited about?

Make a list of the things you want to take on your trip:

- --
- --
- --
- --
- --

Here are the people going with me!

Traveling...

Date:_____

Weather:

What I did today ...

What I loved about today...

Something new I tried or learned today...

Mood:

Write, draw, and collect memories...

Date:_____

Draw, write or stick a ticket, a bill, a map, or anything else you collected from this trip...

After my trip...

Date:_____

How would you rate this trip?

Color the stars...

> 1 star - Didn't like the trip
> 2 stars - It was okay
> 3 stars - Had a fun trip
> 4 stars - Best trip ever!

☆ ☆ ☆ ☆

Would you recommend this trip to a friend?

✓ Check one...

☐ Yes

☐ No

☐ Maybe

Trip # 6

Destination:

_____

_____

_____

_____

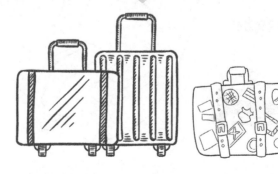

Before the trip...

Date:_____

What are you most excited about?

Make a list of the things you want to take on your trip:

- --

- --

- --

- --

- --

Here are the people going with me!

Traveling...

Date:_____

Weather: ☀ 🌈 ⛅ 🌧 ⛈ 🌨

What I did today ...

What I loved about today...

Something new I tried or learned today...

Mood: 😃 😛 🙂 😐 ☹ 🙁 😮 😴

Write, draw, and collect memories...

Date:_____

Draw, write or stick a ticket, a bill, a map, or anything else you collected from this trip...

After my trip...

Date:_____

How would you rate this trip?

Color the stars...

1 star - Didn't like the trip
2 stars - It was okay
3 stars - Had a fun trip
4 stars - Best trip ever!

Would you recommend this trip to a friend?

✓ Check one...

☐ Yes

☐ No

☐ Maybe

Trip # 7

Destination:

_____

_____

_____

_____

_____

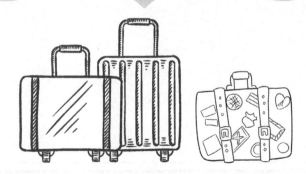

Before the trip...

Date:_____

What are you most excited about?

Make a list of the things you want to take on your trip:

- --
- --
- --
- --
- --

Here are the people going with me!

Traveling...

Date:_____

Weather:

What I did today ...

What I loved about today...

Something new I tried or learned today...

Mood:

Write, draw, and collect memories...

Date:_____

Draw, write or stick a ticket, a bill, a map, or anything else you collected from this trip...

After my trip...

Date:_____

How would you rate this trip?

Color the stars...

1 star - Didn't like the trip
2 stars - It was okay
3 stars - Had a fun trip
4 stars - Best trip ever!

Would you recommend this trip to a friend?

✓ Check one...

☐ Yes

☐ No

☐ Maybe

Trip # 8

Destination:

_____

_____

_____

_____

_____

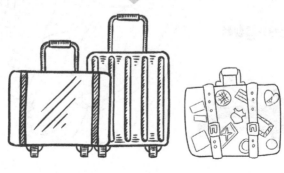

Before the trip...

What are you most excited about?

_____
_____
_____
_____

Make a list of the things you want to take on your trip:

- _____
- _____
- _____
- _____
- _____

Here are the people going with me!

Traveling...

Date:_____

Weather:

What I did today ...

What I loved about today...

Something new I tried or learned today...

Mood:

Date:_____

Draw, write or stick a ticket, a bill, a map, or anything else you collected from this trip...

After my trip...

Date:_____

How would you rate this trip?

Color the stars...

1 star - Didn't like the trip
2 stars - It was okay
3 stars - Had a fun trip
4 stars - Best trip ever!

Would you recommend this trip to a friend?

✓ Check one...

☐ Yes

☐ No

☐ Maybe

Trip # 9

Destination:

_____

_____

_____

_____

_____

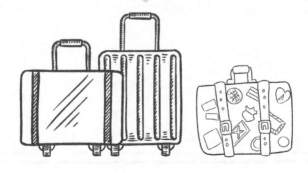

Before the trip...

Date:_____

What are you most excited about?

_____

_____

_____

_____

Make a list of the things you want to take on your trip:

- _____
- _____
- _____
- _____
- _____

Here are the people going with me!

Traveling...

Date:_____

Weather:

What I did today ...

What I loved about today...

Something new I tried or learned today...

Mood:

Draw, write or stick a ticket, a bill, a map, or anything else you collected from this trip...

After my trip...

Date:_____

How would you rate this trip?

Color the stars...

1 star - Didn't like the trip
2 stars - It was okay
3 stars - Had a fun trip
4 stars - Best trip ever!

Would you recommend this trip to a friend?

✓ Check one...

☐ **Yes**

☐ **No**

☐ **Maybe**

Trip # 10

Destination:

_____

_____

_____

_____

_____

Before the trip...

Date:_____

What are you most excited about?

Make a list of the things you want to take on your trip:

- ---------------------------------------
- ---------------------------------------
- ---------------------------------------
- ---------------------------------------
- ---------------------------------------

Here are the people going with me!

Traveling...

Date:_____

Weather: ☀️ 🌈 ⛅ 🌧️ ⛈️ 🌨️

What I did today ...

What I loved about today...

Something new I tried or learned today...

Mood: 😃 😛 🙂 😐 🙁 ☹️ 😮 😴

Write, draw, and collect memories...

Date:_____

Draw, write or stick a ticket, a bill, a map, or anything else you collected from this trip...

After my trip...

Date:_____

How would you rate this trip?

Color the stars...

1 star - Didn't like the trip
2 stars - It was okay
3 stars - Had a fun trip
4 stars - Best trip ever!

Would you recommend this trip to a friend?

✓ Check one...

☐ **Yes**

☐ **No**

☐ **Maybe**

Notes and memories from my trips...

Notes...

Date:__________________

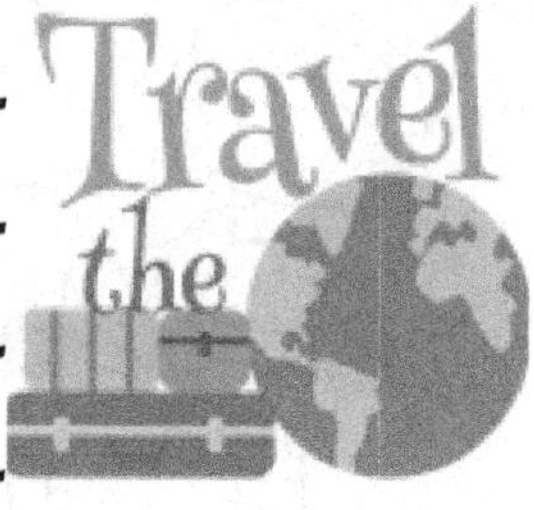

Notes...

Date:_____

Notes...

Travel
the

Notes...

Date:_____

Notes...

Travel
the

Notes...

Travel
the

Notes...

Travel the

Notes...

Date:_____

_____
_____
_____
_____
_____
_____
_____
_____
_____
_____
_____
_____
_____
_____
_____
_____
_____
_____

Travel the

Notes...

Date:_____

Travel the

Notes...

Date:_____

Notes...

Date:_____

Date:_____

Travel the

Notes...

Date:_____

Travel the

Notes...

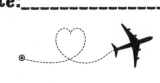

Selfies and other photos from my trips...

Photos...

Photo description...

_____
_____
_____

Photos...

Date:_____

Place:_____

Photo description...

Photos...

Date:_____

Place:_____

Photo description...

_____

_____

_____

Photos...

Date:_____

Place:_____

Photo description...

Photos...

Date:_____

Place:_____

Photo description...

_____

_____

_____

Photos...

Photo description...

Photos...

Photo description...

_____

_____

_____

Photos...

Photo description...

Photos...

Date:_____

Place:_____

Photo description...

_____

_____

_____

Photos...

Date:_____

Place:_____

Photo description...

Photos...

Date:_____

Place:_____

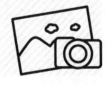

Photo description...

_____

_____

_____

Photos...

Photo description...

_____

_____

_____

Photos...

Photo description...

_____
_____
_____

Photos...

Date:_____

Place:_____

Photo description...

Photos...

Date:_____

Place:_____

Photo description...

Photos...

Photo description...

My dream trip...

Date:_____

Place:_____

If I could go anywhere...

_____
_____
_____
_____
_____
_____
_____
_____
_____
_____
_____
_____
_____
_____
_____
_____
_____
_____

My dream trip...

Date:_____

Place:_____

If I could go anywhere...

_____
_____
_____
_____
_____
_____
_____
_____
_____
_____
_____
_____
_____
_____
_____
_____
_____

My dream trip...

Date:_______________

Place:_______________

If I could go anywhere...

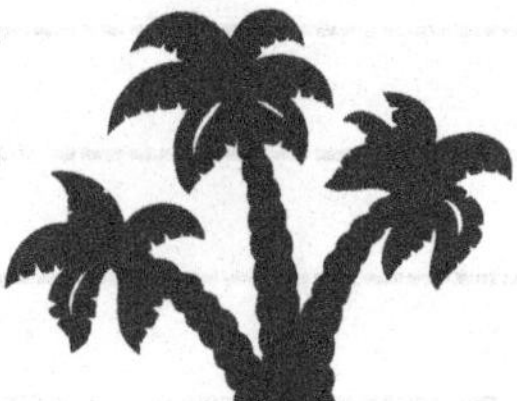

My dream trip...

Date:_____

Place:_____

If I could go anywhere...

_____
_____
_____
_____
_____
_____
_____
_____
_____
_____
_____
_____
_____
_____
_____
_____
_____
_____
_____

My dream trip...

Date:_____

Place:_____

If I could go anywhere...

My dream trip...

Date:________________

Place:_______________

If I could go anywhere...

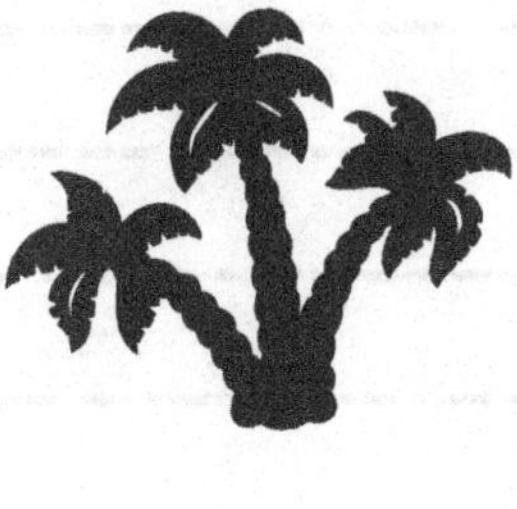

My dream trip...

Date:_____

Place:_____

If I could go anywhere...

My dream trip...

Date:_____

Place:_____

If I could go anywhere...

_____

_____

_____

_____

_____

_____

_____

_____

_____

_____

_____

_____

_____

_____

_____

_____

_____

_____

My dream trip...

Date:_____

Place:_____

If I could go anywhere...

--------------------------------.

My dream trip...

Date:_______________

Place:_______________

If I could go anywhere...

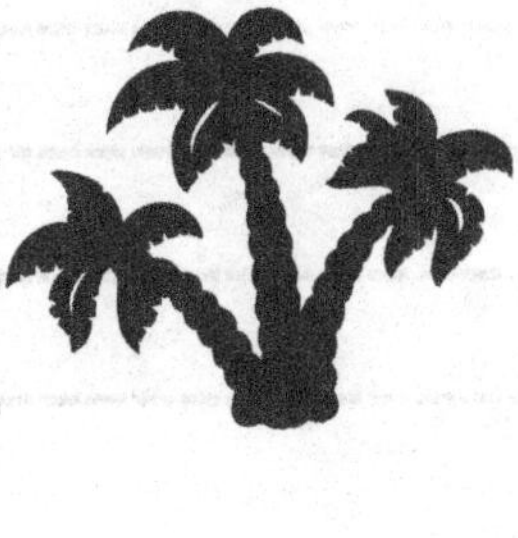

My dream trip...

Date:_____

Place:_____

If I could go anywhere...

My dream trip...

Date:_____

Place:_____

If I could go anywhere...

_____

_____

_____

_____

_____

_____

_____

_____

_____

_____

_____

_____

_____

_____

_____

_____

_____

_____

_____

WHERE TO NEXT?

Made in the USA
Monee, IL
10 June 2025